Confessions of a Self-Published Author

60 Lessons I Wish I Knew Sooner

Jenny Alexander

Jenny Alexander Publishing

Disclaimer: This information reflects the author's personal experience and does not guarantee specific results. Some content may become outdated over time, so please do your own research.

This book was updated on January 7, 2026, to include new information about Goodreads and Amazon's Author Central section.

PS: The eBook version will work best with the Kindle app.

Table of Contents

Preface

When I first began my self-publishing journey, I had no idea what I was doing. I learned everything from the ground up. But I did it. And I'm so glad.

I wrote this book to share many of the lessons I learned, sometimes the hard way. I'm confident this will give you an advantage I didn't have and make your journey smoother.

Sincerely,

Jenny

Introduction

Imagine we are sitting at a coffee shop with a steaming mug of coffee or tea. Imagine we are there with the sole purpose of encouraging each other as indie authors.

As we begin our time together, I ask if you have time for me to share 60 lessons from my journey. You agree, eager to learn from another author. Not even caring if we're at the shop long enough to refill our cups a time or two.

During the chat, I share 60 lessons I learned, things I'd have done differently, and takeaways for your benefit. I'd also share extras like categorized self-publishing tips, do's and don'ts, an indie author timeline, and personal mishaps and wins.

But since we can't actually chat face-to-face, consider this book everything I'd tell you if I could.

And the bonus? You can refer back to it and share it with others.

If you're ready to dive in, turn the page for the first lesson. I'm excited to begin.

By the way, I share a few affiliate links in the following pages. That means if you make a purchase using those links, I'll earn a commission at no extra cost to you. We'll talk more about affiliate partnerships as they relate to self-publishing later.

It's Okay to Break the Rules

Early on, I learned to take advice, even from experts, with a grain of salt. I had to figure out what worked for me.

Because of that, I eventually believed that even if some people said I couldn't format a children's book using Canva, they might not be right. Not following that "rule" helped me successfully self-publish two children's books using Canva.

What I'd Do Differently

I'd spend less time listening to experts and more time experimenting.

Your book doesn't have to look like everyone else's.

Prove the Naysayers Wrong

Many will tell you indie authors shouldn't create their own covers. I disagree. Eventually I learned how easy the design process is. I even created a tutorial on my YouTube channel, which I'll link to in the resources section.

Professionals created some of my covers, but I created more than half of them. The process can be fun and also rewarding.

What I'd Do Differently

I'd explore designing my own cover on Canva sooner.

It's truly possible to create a nice cover design on your own.

Affordable Options, Amazing Results

Some will tell you to set aside hundreds of dollars for a book cover. But that's not necessary. If you don't want to design your own cover but have a small budget, GetCovers can help.

They're based in Ukraine and do amazing work affordably. The most I spent on one of their covers was $50 Canadian. They have cheaper options than that, too.

What I'd Do Differently

I wouldn't have made my first two covers with KDP software initially.

Research your design options thoroughly early on.

Skip the Editor? Maybe.

You may not need an editor. This isn't a popular opinion, but it's true. Especially if you're relatively good with grammar, punctuation, and the English language in general.

I share cost-cutting editing tips in my book *How to Self-Publish on a Shoestring Budget* which I'll link to in the resource section.

What I'd Do Differently

I wouldn't have necessarily hired editors through Fiverr.

Hire an editor only if it's within your budget.

AI: Your Indie Author Assistant

AI is a wonderful tool for the self-published author. It can help with editing or suggest cover and interior formatting designs. If you're creating a kids activity book, AI is a great source for ideas.

It's worthwhile exploring how AI can be of assistance. As long as you're upfront with Amazon about your use of AI, it's allowed.

What I'd Do Differently

I'd have used AI for editing assistance instead of paying for a Fiverr gig.

Ask AI to suggest editorial revisions for your manuscript.

Learn Formatting Skills First

Learn how to format your books before you publish. You don't have to settle for less than stellar interiors.

Formatting is fairly easy with Canva or Microsoft Word, especially since you can find templates on the KDP site or other websites. They're not hard to find with a simple Internet search.

What I'd Do Differently

I wouldn't have settled for inferior interiors early on.

Search out a YouTube tutorial on this topic.

Grace over Perfection Every Time

No matter how much time you spend editing your book, it's likely you'll find a typo or two down the road. This isn't the end of the world, even though some seem to think typos reflect poorly on an author's reputation.

I'm not advocating for sloppy work. I am suggesting we show ourselves grace for the typos that escape our best efforts. A typo or two does not discredit the value of our work.

What I'd Do Differently

I'd have shown myself more grace for typos I found post-publishing.

💡 Don't stress too much about typos. They're easy to fix.

Trust the Story Within You

Popular advice says that you should research whether your book has success potential before you write it. While there is truth to that, I'd argue that it's more important to write the book on your heart.

It's easy to tell when a book is written from the heart. A heartfelt book is more impactful as well.

What I'd Do Differently

I'd have been proud that I'd written from the heart sooner.

Write what's on your heart and don't look back.

Experimentation is the Name of the Game

It's always best to write from the heart, but it's also okay to experiment with different genres. You don't have to stick to just one.

I started experimenting early on. My first six books were non-fiction/self-help. After that, I tried word searches, journals, children's picture books, and activity books. As an indie author, the sky is the limit.

What I'd Do Differently

I'd have experimented more sooner.

Write a list of the different genres you want to self-publish.

Not Everyone Has to Love Your Book

Don't panic if you receive a negative review. And don't go changing your book because someone doesn't like something in it.

Keep these types of comments in perspective. A negative review means you're human and that not everyone is a fan of your work. This is okay. It means you're perfectly normal.

What I'd Do Differently

I wouldn't let a critic rattle me. I'd count it as perfectly normal.

Your book doesn't need another person's approval to be valuable.

Invest Where it Counts

It's okay to have a small budget as a self-published author. It's also okay to make wise investments from time to time. For you, that might mean a Canva membership or splurging on Publisher Rocket, which is a valuable tool that can help you choose appropriate keywords and categories for Amazon KDP.

No matter your budget, I'm certain there are tools that will fit within your constraints.

What I'd Do Differently

I'd have purchased a Canva membership sooner.

Research author tools to decide what'll assist you best.

Author Scams to Avoid

Avoid Bookleaf Publishing's Facebook poetry challenge. It's a scam. I'd also recommend passing on interview requests from Reader's Magnet. While they may seem legitimate at first, they follow up persistently, urging you to spend money to be featured in book fairs.

If something feels too good to be true or sets off your alarm bells, trust your instincts and walk away.

What I'd Do Differently

I would have ignored Bookleaf's poetry challenge and Reader's Magnet.

Resources exist to protect indie authors from scams. Find them.

Revise, Refresh, and then Release

If you don't like something about your book, change it. You can update the cover, the content. Anything. At any time, depending on the platforms you use. That's one of the beautiful things about self-publishing.

I revised most of my first six books, reformatted them, and updated several covers. I felt better about them after doing so.

What I'd Do Differently

I'd have revised my first few books sooner.

💡 Feel free to make changes. Check the platform rules first.

Silence Your Inner Critic

Your inner critic will try to convince you your work isn't good enough. This is a common struggle for authors. Decide not to make decisions based on self-doubt.

Having supportive friends, family, or an online community helps when that doubt gets loud. Knowing this struggle is normal also helps.

What I'd Do Differently

I'd have spent less time criticizing my work.

Understand early that feelings of self-doubt are normal.

Small Wins Deserve Big Cheers

One way to combat your inner critic is by celebrating small wins. Did you get a sale? A positive review? Make a difference to someone with your writing? Celebrate it.

You can do this simply. Tell a friend, share it on your social media page, or treat yourself to something.

What I'd Do Differently

I'd have focused more on the small wins and less on the self-doubt.

Make a list of ways you'd like to celebrate all the small wins.

KDP Issues You Shouldn't Ignore

I mentioned earlier that some rules are meant to be broken. There are others that should be followed closely like not doing review swaps with other authors. It's also important to choose book categories on Amazon that accurately reflect your content. Otherwise, Amazon may not approve your book.

Learn what's expected. Connecting with an author community can help you stay informed.

What I'd Do Differently

I'd have congratulated myself for saying no to a review swap.

Learn the rules of publishing platforms like Amazon.

You Don't Have to Write Alone

Writing can be lonely. That's why finding a community is important. I found Facebook to be better for this than Instagram.

If you haven't already, create an Instagram or Facebook author page and start connecting with others. Want your first author connection? Feel free to follow me: Jenny Alexander, Author at https:// www.facebook.com/hopefortheheartroken

What I'd Do Differently

I'd have found other authors online sooner.

Sign up for the social media platform most appealing to you.

Stand Out from the Crowd

Will you use a pen name or your real name? Either way, check if another author is already using it. If so, adding your middle initial will help you stand out.

Be consistent regardless of the name you choose. Some authors use different names for different genres, but I haven't. And neither has the other Jenny Alexander!

What I'd Do Differently

I'd have used the name Jenny E. Alexander for all of my books.

💡 Search for the name you want to use on Amazon.

Goodreads On My Mind

Goodreads.com is another place to find a community and collect reviews. If your book is on Amazon, it should show up there automatically.

That's another reason to make sure your author name is unique, your books could show up under someone else's profile! This has happened to me.

What I'd Do Differently

I'd have created a Goodreads account using my middle initial.

> Ensure someone else isn't using the same name as you.

To Respond or Not? That's the Question.

If you receive a review on Goodreads, you have the option of responding. The funny thing is since publishing this book, I learned that Goodreads may ban authors from replying to their own reviews. Though I wasn't banned, they warned me I could be if I replied to one of my reviews again.

Always check the rules on the platforms you join to make sure you know what's permitted.

What I'd Do Differently

I wouldn't have commented on my reviews at all had I known this sooner.

💡 Do your research to find out what's allowed on platforms.

Market on a Shoestring Budget

Most of us don't have big budgets for marketing, and that's okay. You can promote your book for free or nearly free.

Social media is one way. Another? Place your book in a free little library near you. There are countless creative ideas out there. To find more, just do a quick Internet search.

What I'd Do Differently

I'd have spent more time marketing my books creatively sooner.

💡 Make a list of the marketing methods that appeal to you.

Your Strategy, Your Pace

Many authors swear by having an email list. It's a good idea but not a requirement, at least in my opinion.

I started mine late and only have 10 subscribers. I'm not consistent sending them, either.

In short, do what works for you, not necessarily what everyone else is doing.

What I'd Do Differently

I may not have even started a newsletter.

Decide what's best for you without pressure from others.

Don't Rush Your Masterpiece

I may have rushed the process of my first books. It's always better to take your time. You'll be happier with the final product sooner.

I watched my husband self-publish his two books. He didn't rush but didn't delay either. In the end, he was happy was the final product in a way that I wasn't. I recommend learning from his example rather than mine.

What I'd Do Differently

I'd have taken more time with my first few books.

Be patient as you go through the process. You won't regret it.

Fantastic Facebook Finds

Facebook groups can be a goldmine for indie authors. One especially helpful group for me was Women Writers, Editors, Agents, and Publishers (WWEAP) : https://www.facebook.com/groups/wweap.

Through it, I scored a free beta read and free editing services. That said, the replies in the group can be snarky, so I didn't stick around. Still, the value I received was undeniable.

What I'd Do Differently

I may have ignored the group snarkiness and stuck around.

Search for private Facebook groups or join WWEAP.

Choose Your Community Wisely

Early in my journey, I joined public Facebook groups for authors. But most of them were flooded with spam. While that might not be true for every public group, it was enough of a red flag for me to step away.

As I mentioned earlier, having a community of fellow authors is valuable. Facebook groups can provide that, but public groups tend to have more spam than private ones.

What I'd Do Differently

I wouldn't have bothered joining public Facebook groups.

💡 Be selective about the public Facebook groups you join.

The Free Challenge Funnel

I participated in a Facebook challenge for authors not long after self-publishing my first book. The host, Jasmine Wommack, provided valuable insights, and I learned a lot. It was a great experience until the sales pitch.

I came to understand that many of these challenges lead into a high-ticket offer. The pressure to buy can be intense. I didn't fall for it, but felt the stress.

What I'd Do Differently

I'd have been prepared for the high pressure sales pitch.

Join the challenges you like knowing why they exist.

Audience First, Course Second

During Jasmine's Facebook challenge, I learned that authors can create courses based on their books. Inspired, I jumped in and built one, then uploaded it to my website.

But I didn't have much of an audience at the time so didn't sell a single course. A few kind acquaintances took it for free and gave helpful feedback. But I learned that creating the course so soon wasn't the best use of my time.

What I'd Do Differently

I would've focused on refining and promoting my book.

💡 Consider if now is the best time for course creation.

Crack the Book Title Code

During Jasmine's Facebook challenge, I learned a simple formula for titling non-fiction books:

- Main Title = the core outcome for the reader
- Subtitle = what the reader will learn or gain

I tried to use that formula with this book and my others. It seems to simplify the title and subtitle creation process.

What I'd Do Differently

I would've used this formula from the very beginning.

Practice this formula with your book title ideas.

Before You Buy a Domain, Read This

In my first year as an indie author, I tried Wix and purchased the premium plan, thinking I needed it to host my video course. The next year, I renewed with a cheaper package. But by year three, I let it go entirely.

While the idea of having an author website sounded great, I received more spam than benefits. The traffic wasn't worth the cost.

What I'd Do Differently

I wouldn't have invested in a website so early.

💡 Consider the pros and cons of a website.

Platform Hopping Isn't a Crime

One of the most freeing parts of being an indie author is the ability to experiment with platforms. I tried KDP, Draft2Digital, Uncursed, and Gumroad. When some of those platforms didn't deliver results, I removed my books. Later, I tried one of them again, and it worked better. That was Gumroad, by the way.

The takeaway? It's okay to test, tweak, and change your mind.

What I'd Do Differently

I would've taken more time upfront to research my publishing options.

> Determine early what platforms you'd like to try.

Reaching Readers Your Way

As I said earlier, many experts say authors need a newsletter. While that may be true, there are other options. Two that come to mind are Substack and Medium.

I tried Substack without success but have done well on Medium. Readers seem to like what I say about self-publishing so I've built an audience there. The bonus is I get paid to write since I'm in their partner program.

What I'd Do Differently

I'd have written about my self-publishing journey sooner.

💡 Try platforms like Substack or Medium and see what works.

Link Platforms Like a Pro

When I relaunched my Gumroad account, I focused exclusively on listing my self-publishing books and linked the store to my Medium profile. That simple connection has led to several sales.

If you write within a specific niche and become known for it, consider linking your platforms strategically. Cross-promoting in this way can help boost sales.

What I'd Do Differently

I would've waited to set up Gumroad until I established myself on Medium.

Consider linking several platforms.

Win Hearts, Not Just Sales

Whether you're writing for Medium, Substack, or elsewhere, your readers want more than a pitch, they want connection. When you offer genuine value and personal insight, readers are more likely to stick around, engage with, and support your work.

Linking your products at the end of your articles is like a gentle nudge so readers know they're there.

What I'd Do Differently

I wish I had started sharing heartfelt self-publishing lessons sooner.

Share your heart and experiences with your readers.

Every Review is a Wonderful Gift

No matter where your books are sold, reviews matter. They add social proof. Always include a request for reviews at the end of your books and occasionally post a friendly reminder on social media.

If acquaintances buy your book, ask them to leave a review. You can also reach out to book bloggers who specialize in your genre. They're often happy to help.

What I'd Do Differently

I would've appreciated the reviews I'd received, even though I wanted more.

Put in some effort trying to get reviews for your book(s).

Let a Trusted Voice Lift Yours

Editorial reviews can lend credibility, but they often come with a high price tag. If it's in your budget, go for it. If not, try Readersfavorite.com. Their free option won't guarantee a review, but if selected, won't cost you a thing.

Also consider Facebook contests. I won an editorial review through a Facebook contest. Keep your eyes open for similar opportunities.

What I'd Do Differently

I would've signed up for a free review from Readers Favorite sooner.

💡 Fill in Readers Favorite's form for a free review.

Follow the Leaders, Learn from the Pros

There's a wealth of wisdom out there from experienced self-published authors. Some of my favorites are Dale L. Roberts, J.F. Penn, and Wendy H. Jones.

Investing in their books, whether eBooks or paperbacks, can help you grow faster and avoid common pitfalls.

What I'd Do Differently

I would've chosen one or two authors instead of reading from so many.

Start building your own library of trusted resources.

Stop the Noise of Too Many Voices

Learning from others is crucial, but listening to too many people can lead to overwhelm. One author might say "do this," while another says, "do the opposite." That conflicting advice can burn you out.

Choose one or two mentors whose style and philosophy align with yours. Stick with them when you're starting out.

What I'd Do Differently

I wouldn't have learned from so many authors, at least in the beginning.

💡 Decide which authors you want to learn from.

Social Media Overwhelm?

Social media is a great tool for the indie author. It's a wonderful way to connect with fellow authors and potential readers. But I've heard it's not necessary to be on every platform. Picking one or two is plenty.

I started with a Facebook author page and eventually tried Instagram. But it seemed too much to keep up with. Now, I stick with Facebook and that's just right for me.

What I'd Do Differently

I wouldn't have tried Instagram since Facebook already worked for me.

Pick your social media platform of choice.

Avoid Spam While Staying Connected

My Facebook author page is constantly flooded with spam messages. Almost all the direct messages I receive are spam. I typically don't respond but block and delete the profiles.

You could combat this by going into the Messages section of Meta and setting up an automated response using the "Automations" feature. This is something I've done more recently.

What I'd Do Differently

I would have set up an automated message much sooner.

> Decide how you'd like to deal with spam messages.

Handling Account Deletion Warnings

If you receive one, or multiple, account deletion notifications, rest assured they're spam. You haven't broken any rules. I've received more of these than I can count. Now, I simply block and delete them.

Usually, the profiles sending these messages don't even have a proper profile photo, rather a symbol.

What I'd Do Differently

I would have ignored these account deletion warnings sooner.

💡 Learn to recognize and ignore suspicious messages.

Posting with Purpose on Social Meda

Whether you're on Facebook, Instagram, or Twitter, aim to add value for your followers. Avoid constantly pushing your book links.

A strategy I learned involves sharing different types of posts on different days. For example:
- Monday: Book quote
- Tuesday: Personal photo
- Wednesday: Indie author tip

You can tailor your schedule to your genre.

What I'd Do Differently

I would have developed a social media strategy much earlier. I still need one!

Decide what kind of content you want to share. Plan ahead.

Stronger Boundaries, Stronger You

Setting boundaries is a powerful and necessary tool. If you need to say no, do so. You do not even need to explain yourself. After all, you cannot do everything. It is best to prioritize what is important and let go of the rest.

I have gotten better at saying no. It is less of a struggle now, and for that, I am glad.

What I'd Do Differently

I would have said no more often instead of saying yes.

💡 Give yourself permission to "just say no".

Count the Wins, Not the Woes

Gratitude is a great antidote to discouragement. Maybe you hoped for more book sales or reviews. Instead of focusing on that, be thankful for what you do have. That shift in perspective reminds you of the progress you've made.

I've gone through periods of lower book sales and unmet expectations, but remembering my wins helped me stay motivated.

What I'd Do Differently

I would have focused more on what I had instead of what I lacked.

Write a list of your self-publishing wins.

Define Success on Your Terms

Self-publishing is a business, and businesses are built on sales. At the same time, it's a good idea to come up with your own definition of success. It often means more than earnings.

For a lot of us indie authors, we earn modestly. And that's okay. Success has different definitions. For me, I'm thankful with the earnings I've received and for the business that I built from scratch.

What I'd Do Differently

I would have enjoyed the journey more.

Come up with your own definition of success.

Get Booked on Podcasts

Podcasts are a powerful and free way to market your book. Don't let the myth that they're hard to find hold you back. In fact, Facebook groups simplify the process.

A great group to start with is:
 https://
www.facebook.com/groups/podcastguestcolla
boration

What I'd Do Differently

I wouldn't have believed that podcast opportunities were hard to come by.

Start exploring podcast opportunities.

From Nervous to a Natural

I'm an introvert at heart, but I became more comfortable with podcasts through consistent practice.

Even if the idea of being interviewed terrifies you, give it a shot. You might be surprised at how quickly your confidence builds. Besides, most podcast hosts are pros at helping their guests feel at ease.

What I'd Do Differently

I'd have given myself grace for being nervous.

You don't have to be perfect, just be willing to start.

Build a Podcast Porfolio

Podcasts can boost your author credibility. That's because they help others learn about your story and why you wrote your books.

If you have a website, podcasts can also increase your visibility. Hosts often link to your social media or website. Likewise, you can showcase all of your appearances on your website.

What I'd Do Differently

As soon as I started podcast interviews, I'd have posted them on my website.

💡 Document your podcast journey from the first episode.

Stay Organized with a Podcast Schedule

Once podcast interviews start rolling in, create a schedule. It doesn't matter if that schedule is on a spreadsheet or your phone. And, once you have that schedule, review it often.

I missed one interview because I didn't double-check my calendar. I apologized to the host, but I never heard back from him. It was a tough lesson, and I regret not being more diligent.

What I'd Do Differently

I'd have reviewed my interview calendar weekly or every few days.

Respect every opportunity, and be diligent about your schedule.

Value Rest Over Momentum

At one point, I had nearly back-to-back podcast interviews for an entire month. It was thrilling, and my confidence soared, but eventually I burned out.

The interview I missed? It was scheduled a month later than the others, and I completely forgot about it. That was a symptom that I needed rest.

What I'd Do Differently

I wouldn't have scheduled that last interview. I'd have prioritized a break.

💡 Even when momentum builds, protect your energy.

Shine through Written Interviews

If podcasting isn't your thing, consider written interviews. Sites like AwesomeGang.com and Bold Journey magazine offer great opportunities.

You can showcase these interviews on your author website just like podcasts. They'll build your credibility in a similar way.

What I'd Do Differently

I'd have added my written interviews to my website sooner.

Search for written interview opportunities.

No Website? No Problem.

Can't afford a custom domain? Start with a free blog on platforms like Blogger.

Create posts for your interviews, book lists, reviews, and more.

I eventually realized that affordability doesn't have to mean lack of web presence. Check out my author blog here: https://www.blogger.com/profile/09547633116391529064

What I'd Do Differently

I probably wouldn't have used Wix during my first two years.

💡 Consider what your budget will allow, and make a plan.

Divide and Conquer Your Inbox

I recommend setting up a dedicated email address specifically for your book business.

I did this early on and have no regrets. While I occasionally used my personal email for business matters, I generally kept the two communication streams separate. This helped me stay organized and maintain boundaries.

What I'd Do Differently

I'd be stricter about keeping my personal and business emails separate.

💡 Set up a separate email address for your author business.

Plan Your Business, Plan Your Breaks

You don't necessarily need a separate planner for your book business, but you may want one. Regardless, I recommend roughly planning out your schedule from day to day. Be sure to include breaks.

It's far too easy to work around the clock, especially when you're doing something you enjoy.

What I'd Do Differently

Looking back, I wish I had taken more breaks from the beginning.

💡 Block out time for your work and your breaks.

Monitor Your Money, It Matters

Since your books are a business, it's important to develop the habit of tracking your expenses and earnings early on. A simple spreadsheet will do the job.

I use one spreadsheet specifically for expenses where I record each purchase and its cost. In a separate spreadsheet, I track all of my earnings. They include book sales, affiliate earnings, and other income.

What I'd Do Differently

I'd have given myself credit for tracking finances from the beginning.

Choose a system or program that works best for you.

What Self-Publishing Really Costs

As I've mentioned before, self-publishing doesn't have to break the bank. In fact, for several of my books, the only expense was the proof copy. That cost is minimal. And it's always worth it, especially when publishing in a new genre.

For my first children's book, I needed two proof copies before getting it right. I was so glad I took the time to perfect it.

What I'd Do Differently

Early on, I likely would have limited my expenses to only the proof copy.

Decide your budget, and stick to it.

Lend a Helping Hand to Other Authors

Whether you've self-published one book or fifty, you have valuable experience that others may not have. You're now in a position to help someone else on their journey.

Maybe a friend or family member could use guidance. If you have the time and willingness, offering support can be incredibly rewarding. After all, you were once in their shoes. Helping another is a sign of how much you've grown.

What I'd Do Differently

I may have offered to help a fellow author out sooner.

💡 Be open-minded when it comes to supporting indie authors..

Help Wisely, Not Widely

It's perfectly fine not to help someone who isn't a friend or family member. You can't be everyone's go-to person.

For example, a connection on Medium asked me for a consultation, and I said no. However, I did help my husband and mother-in-law with their books.

What I'd Do Differently

I'd have prepared myself sooner for others needing my help in the future.

Consider who you might help down the road.

Multiple Streams, More Stability

As you probably know, most authors do not typically make a full-time income from their books. Because of that, I recommend diversifying your income.

You might try writing blog posts on Substack or Medium, or sharing affiliate links for products you have tried. I found success on Medium and with my Publisher Rocket affiliate link. I also earn money by taking online surveys.

What I'd Do Differently

I'd have diversified my income sooner.

Search for income streams that appeal to you.

If It Doesn't Work, Let it Go

As I mentioned, I've had success with affiliate links. But only for Publisher Rocket. I tried the affiliate partnership for another company but getting paid was harder than it should have been, so I let it go.

Don't be afraid to let an income stream go if it's not working as well as it should. There's always something else to try.

What I'd Do Differently

I'd have looked into why I wasn't getting paid from the company sooner.

💡 Be prepared to let opportunities that don't work for you go.

Celebrate Your Supportive Circle

While we hope to reach new readers, the encouragement and book purchases from those closest to us is something to count as a blessing.

Both my husband and I have had that support. If you don't yet, I urge you to find your community. Truly, the authors on Facebook encourage and support each other. It's worth checking out.

What I'd Do Differently

I'd have appreciated friend and family support sooner.

Appreciate those who support you or find a community.

Extras for Your Journey

Tips for
INDIE AUTHORS

1. Cover Design

- For inspiration, see what other covers in your genre look like.
- Always test your thumbnail. Know that it'll be a smaller size every time.

2. Book Interior

- Full justify the text in your manuscript.
- Use page breaks before each new chapter (in Microsoft Word)
- Use the style feature (in Microsoft Word) for headings.
- Add page numbers and a clickable Table of Contents (for eBooks). Check the Reference section of Word.

3. Metadata

- Add seven keywords in your KDP dashboard that readers would search for.

- Choose categories beyond just the obvious. Use less competitive ones using tools like Publisher Rocket or Amazon's own category search.

- If you'd like to purchase Publisher Rocket, you're welcome to copy and paste my link into your browser: https://publisherrocket.com/?affiliate=5books

4. Amazon Author Page

- Set up your Amazon Author Central page with a bio, photo.

5. Content Marketing

- Repurpose a section of your book into a blog post.
- Create a series of social media quotes from your book using Canva.
- Record a reel about your writing process or publishing tips.
- Create a series of short videos based on each chapter of your book.
- Post a mockup of your book cover for social media using Canva.

6. Additional Income Ideas

You can get paid to do surveys. Get started by using my affiliate links:

PrizeRebel: https://www.prizerebel.com/index.php?r=15503513

Branded Surveys: https://surveys.gobranded.com/users/register/JAL75232

The Indie Author Journey
A VISUAL TIMELINE

1 **The Spark**
A dream, an idea, or a message you can't ignore.

2 **Planning & Plotting**
Brainstorming, creating outlines (or not).

3 **Writing the First Draft**
Putting words to a page, maybe messy but always real.

4 **Editing & Revisions**
Refining your work with fresh eyes and maybe tears.

5 **Formatting & Design**
Interior layout, cover creation, etc.

6 **Publishing Day**
Your book baby is officially out in the world!

7 **Marketing & Reviews**
Spreading the word, collecting social proof from reviews.

8 **The Growth Phase**
Building your brand, writing more books, always learning.

9 **Looking Back**
Reflecting on how far you've come.

Wins & Losses from
MY JOURNEY

Someone watched my interview with Gretchen Baskerville, appreciated my story, and sent me a thoughtful email. I accidentally deleted it, but she graciously resent it.

Grace in action

I self-published a book with a typo on the cover. Thankfully, someone pointed it out, and I corrected it.

Progress over perfection

After a podcast interview, I realized I needed to clarify something I'd said. The host kindly updated the show notes with the correction.

Own mistakes

Early on, I looked into contributing to an anthology. But the high cost to write a single chapter felt like a red flag. I chose not to participate.

Trust the gut

Wins & Losses from
MY JOURNEY

There were many times I worked late into the evening because I hadn't built breaks into my schedule.

Balance is key

I wasted hours struggling with formatting in the beginning. Then I learned how to properly use Microsoft Word and Canva for creating interiors.

Research options first

I finally got one of my books in a local bookstore but there have been no sales as far as I know.

Monitor expectations

I said no to a paid radio interview before I learned that all interviews should be offered free of charge.

Be careful

Epilogue

The behind-the-scenes glimpses I've given you could only come by experience. But guess what? No matter how long it's been since you published your first book, you have experience too.

Let that really sink in and encourage you. That experience means that even if you're not where you want to be, you're not where you were.

That's something to be proud of and remember when you feel discouraged.

We all get discouraged from time to time. But we keep going. And that's what matters.

Review Request

If this book made a difference in your self-publishing journey, would you take a few moments to leave a brief written review? I read every one. They mean so much and help others find my work. Thank you in advance.

Resources

1. Cover Design Instructional Tutorial: https://youtu.be/-G_XzgBEl-w
2. How to Self-Publish on a Shoestring Budget: savvyselfpublishing.gumroad.com/l/lphul
3. Bookleaf Publishing Scam: https://medium.com/p/5c5b01c145d6
4. Reader's Magnet Scam: https://youtu.be/hIS7nbcm7xc

About the Author

Jenny Alexander has self-published over 25 books in multiple genres. Most of her books have a common theme of imparting hope and inspiration from a faith-based perspective. Others, like her activity books, are simply for fun. This is her third book about self-publishing.

She lives in Ontario, Canada, with her husband Curtis. In her spare time she loves pursuing various creative endeavours like art and music.

www.ingramcontent.com/pod-product-compliance
Lightning Source LLC
Chambersburg PA
CBHW060645210326
41520CB00010B/1744